Crossing State Lines

Crossing State Lines

Poems by Joseph A. Chelius

Word Poetry

Published by Word Poetry
P.O. Box 541106
Cincinnati, OH 45254-1106

ISBN: 9781625493446

Poetry Editor: Kevin Walzer
Business Editor: Lori Jareo

Visit us on the web at www.wordpoetrybooks.com

Acknowledgments

I am grateful to the editors of the following publications in which many of these poems have appeared:

Blue Unicorn: "Leaving the Editor's Shop"

Drexel Online Journal: "Haircut on My Fortieth Birthday," "In Denim"

Moonstone Poetry Anthology: "Van Loading"

Poet Lore: "On Watching Replays of a Pitcher Struck in the Face by a Comeback Line Drive"

Rattle: "Stockboy"

r.kv.ry: "Old Man"

Schuylkill Valley Journal: "At Five Points," "Before the Eagles Game," "Brown Moth on Windshield," "City Church Bells at Dusk," "Face," "For My Troubled Prostate, St. Peregrine Arrives," "Layoff," "New Primer for Boys," "Purge," "Santa, Delayed," "Saturday Chores with Jehovah's Witnesses," "To My Well-Behaved Self," "To the Elderly Parishioner I Found Hemorrhaging in the Church Yard"

Spitball: "Not Cooperstown"

The American Journal of Poetry: "Cleaning Up After the Nar-Anon Family Group Meeting," "Crossing State Line," "Soda Machine at the Garrett Road Laundromat," "Straightening the Garage," "White Rambler, Last Ride"

U.S. 1 Worksheets: "After Writing," "House Hunting in the Suburbs During the Jetson Years," "Rock Zealots in My Religion Class," "Validation"

"Face," "Haircut on My Fortieth Birthday," and "In Denim" were reprinted in *Taking Pitches,* Pudding House Chapbook Series, 2006; "Leaving the Editor's Shop" was reprinted in *Row House Yards,* Pudding House Chapbook Series, 2011.

Cover photograph: Patricia Griffin-Chelius

Proofreading: Sharyl Wolf

With gratitude to the Bucks County, Pennsylvania, poet laureate program and the Bucks County community of poets, especially Bill Wunder and Bernadette McBride, poetry editors of *Schuylkill Valley Journal;* my LaSalle University writing friends (Tim Walters, Joe Boyce, and David Livewell) for their years of friendship and correspondence; and poet and mentor Christopher Bursk, master sorter of baseball cards.

For my mother, my father, and my siblings and their families; for Patricia, Sarah, and Andrew...fellow travelers across the state lines.

"Try on your brother's coat for size. Maybe walk a mile in his shoes."
—James C. Fallon
  LaSalle University philosophy professor

Table of Contents

III. Brown Duster

I. Aquamarine Station Wagon

Not Cooperstown

Go in early June, a Sunday morning,
when traffic on the Turnpike is light.
Knock politely at the house
his parents sold in Delaware County,
and when the owners shrug and let you in
take the stairs as he once did—
two at a time to the third-floor bedroom
where the fleece pennant of dancing Snoopy
remains tacked to the closet door.
Move aside the manual typewriter
with the twisted ribbon.
Among the unlabeled cassettes,
a year's subscription to *Mad* magazine,
you'll find the relics of a faded league:
chipped dice, baseball cards from the late 1960s,
records in a spiral notebook of games he staged
fielding teams without a catcher, the corner outfielders,
smudged rubber bands so brittle
they'll disintegrate in your fingers.
Peruse those implausible statistics:
Ferguson Jenkins with his swollen ERA;
muscular Rich Hebner who dug graves in the off-season,
first in infield hits.
Seek out the boy himself who on the rumpled field
of his bed would devote whole afternoons
to rolling snake-eyes for strike out,
pair of sixes for a home run.
Think of that lackadaisical student who never had his art supplies
keeping track of every ground out and pop up,
hidden away where he never had to
respond in class to questions about the amoeba,
nor cycle past the neighborhood kids

as they sat on a curb and fooled with sticks,
waiting for someone to taunt.
Consider his various roles:
statistician, skipper of every team,
capricious commissioner who one day vanished
from the league he'd founded
and entered a dicier world.

Purge

As I lay sick in bed my eyes in a restless orbit
kept turning to the United States presidents
as somber as jurors peering down from the wall—
from Washington to Lyndon Johnson listening
for the doctor to trudge up the stairs
and into the sick room with his gleaming instruments—
cold stethoscope, probing thermometer—
in a worn black kit.

Such authority he exuded full of brusque jokes
and priestly power, scribbling on a tablet,
my mother like a dutiful parishioner
left to abide by those archaic remedies
of enemas and alcohol sponge baths—
spoon bitter medicine around the clock.

And next morning in that emptied house
to appear in her pale robe
and once more place a hand on my forehead,
remove the wadded tissues, bring ginger ale.
She'd stack the hi-fi downstairs
with vinyl crackling like fat on a stove—
songs from *The King & I* and *The Scottish Soldier,*
Christmas music out of season,
The Little Drummer Boy as if leading a purge,
cutting through the mist
of the humidifier, Vicks VapoRub,
softening the countenance of Millard Fillmore,
bearded Benjamin Harrison—presidents
in their imperious order,
aloof, preoccupied with national concerns
while my mother tended a boy in bed.

House Hunting in the Suburbs During the Jetson Years

"Meet George Jetson..." opening theme lyrics from *The Jetsons*, an animated 1960's sitcom

Meet my father, perturbed, as he taps the brakes
in Saturday traffic—
his worn Thom McAn's inserting commas
before we'd come to a stop.
And my mother beside him with sketchy directions,
the yellow puke bucket rattling on the seat.

Consider the confining capsule
of our Chevy station wagon, aquamarine,
its manual steering and bench seats;
in the warm cross-breeze the six of us
elbow-gouging, arguing over territory,
unsettled by talk at dinner
about venturing from our changing neighborhood—
the row house games of step-ball, sock-it-out—

into these remote regions along West Chester Pike
with its strip malls and fast food restaurants,
the car dealerships with fluttery pennants
to cheer us on as we'd enter Utopias
called Falconcrest, Highspire—
places those shrewd developers,
who knew their business,
might have named for white flight itself.

Photo of My Father, Senior High Principal, in Sheriff's Hat and Badge

Hard to suppose it had been
his idea. Not my father,
who all through the '70s
kept his hair short
and sideburns trimmed;
who on Saturday mornings—
the old station wagon
like a faithful steed—
rode into town
with his coupons and list.

But above the witty caption
some yearbook staffer
had penned about
sheriff and posse,
rounding up the school's
bad dudes and outlaws,

I was surprised to see him
(beyond a slight unease
around the eyes) bringing off
this insouciant pose: thumbs
hooked in waistband,
white hat tilted back,

and on the adjoining pages
the unlikely posse
of custodians and secretaries,
cafeteria ladies in hairnets,

his deputy the assistant principal—

Weeble-shaped Mr. Fitzpatrick—
feet crossed on the desk.

Egdorf

We heard his name so often at dinner
it took on the flavor
of some unpalatable food.
Egdorf, my father would snap
while forking up turnips
or spearing meat.
Even the Jane Parker pies
he bought on sale at A&P
turned into Egdorf,
that undermining superintendent,
as we stared at our plates
and tried not to laugh
because the name sounded funny,
and what could we know
of our father's life
as senior high principal,
full to overflowing
with students and faculty,
the new mortgage, six kids?
Fidgety, wanting to be excused,
we left him recounting
for my mother and grandmother—
red-faced, glowering,
the day's dollop of Egdorf
piled on his plate.

Brands

The Sears robe,
the trebly Zenith,

the Kellogg's bran flakes
he took in with the news

on KYW—my father
first down, first done,

leaving us slumped at the table
over bowls and spoons;

then in jacket and tie,
a waft of Old Spice,

returning to place in the sink
that last swallow

of Maxwell House drip
in the enamel cup

I sipped from once,
savoring the dark taste

on my tongue while
through the kitchen window

came the muffled cough
of the Chevy station wagon

he drove to the high school,
the second job at A&P;

those nights home late
with two for one

on Stroehmann white
for the brown bag lunches

he packed before bed—
crisp, in clean uniforms,

that stood at assembly
from September to June.

Batting in Little League

He'd hated the wobbly helmet,
those foam ear flaps
damp from other kids' sweat.

And the bat with some
slugger's name on the label:
Boog Powell, Harmon Killebrew,

hulking first basemen
no one would have told
to move closer or choke up.

How hostile it had always seemed:
the collusion between
pitcher and catcher

as they'd conspire against you;
the impartiality
of the crouching umpire,

his chest protector thrust out
like an indifferent heart.
Legs shaking, malaise spreading

to his shoulders and arms,
he'd watch pitches go by,
squint into the setting sun

at the marooned base runners
on their tiny rafts,
so touching

in their eagerness for home
he'd grip the bat like a heavy oar
and choke up.

To My Well-Behaved Self

Nagging kid brother, my respectable twin,
how I resented those sidelong glances,
your empathy for the sales clerks
as my friends and I raced up the down escalators,
sprayed one another with Jean Nate.
Boy with good manners, your shirt tucked in—
no wonder I tried to ditch you in housewares,
leave you lagging in revolving doors.

But later, in the dark sanctuary of my bedroom,
I'd welcome you like the friend
it embarrassed me to be seen with,
the two of us with sound
lowered on the cheap stereo,
its light a glowing altar,
each song a mumbled prayer.

Friend who never turned on me,
how I appreciated your abiding loyalty—
no snickering, no divulging of secrets
when I'd ease up the volume
to Led Zeppelin's "Stairway to Heaven,"
The Who's "Behind Blue Eyes,"
my voice hesitant until you'd nod encouragement—
the only time all day.

New Primer for Boys

"I hate fist fights. I don't mind getting hit so much—although I'm not crazy about it, naturally—but what scares me most in a fist fight is the guy's face. I can't stand looking at the other guy's face, is my trouble."
—Holden Caulfield, *The Catcher in the Rye*

There are no coaches here,
no men clapping on the baselines
for you to be a hitter
or to look alive in a wilting sun.
With stoicism by the wayside, feel free
to step aside for the sizzling grounder.
Let the burly fullback
push past you like a curtain
as you cheer his dash up-field.

At the window on rainy days,
show pity for all things:
a broken cap pistol;
your sister's doll left lying in a puddle.
Give in to your quiet penchant at dinner
for imagining string beans
as forlorn siblings, a platoon in fatigues
looking for refuge by the stony potatoes
on the side of your plate.

At your next fist fight
be amenable to pulling punches.
Be the budding poet or horticulturist,
unwilling to smash the perfect petals
of another's lips.

To the Elderly Parishioner I Found Hemorrhaging in the Church Yard

How resourceful of me in that time before cell phones
to run to church
where Monsignor in a black cassock
was molding into altar boys
a slouching row of indifferent eighth graders—
boys who preferred nothing better on Saturday mornings
than to scrap on the courts with hockey sticks.

And how impressed you might have been
by my self-restraint, holding by the strings
a box of assorted bakery cookies
while Monsignor, with a heavy patience,
edified at the tabernacle—
raising the gold chalice and intoning in the voice
he used for sermons.

God provides, it can be said with certainty,
so it would have pleased you to know
that He'd chosen as messenger
a boy trained by the Sisters of the Immaculate Heart

to murmur a prayer when an ambulance passed,
nod deferentially at every mention of Jesus,
who stood among the stained glass depictions
of the Stations of the Cross
like a respectful servant or customer in line,

unwilling to call out
(at least not without putting up his hand)
to a priest during the holy tutorial of boys
whose brutal slap shots lifted off asphalt,

whose shrill oaths resounded off buildings—
boys bold, brazen, quick to speak out of turn—
the wrong sorts of messenger
whom God might have sent.

Rock Zealots in My Religion Class

There were a few who sat around me:
Zeppelin freaks and Yes fanatics,
avid readers of the gospel
according to *Rolling Stone*.
"Who is the greatest among us?"
the disciples of Jesus once asked,
and I don't suppose
they'd been referring to Frippertronics
or to three-chord George of the Delaware Destroyers.
Even Dave the bassoonist had the glow,
pushing on me like a glossy prospectus
the work of Emerson Lake & Palmer,
their name solid and respectable—
like a good investment firm's.

But looking back I can only admire
such single-minded devotion:
all the young dudes who dreamed of stardom,
sketching Stratocasters
in the margins of their notebooks,
staying up to learn chords;
the evangelicalism of Patrick Coughlin,
patron of Bonner High's outdoor courts,
sitting red-eyed by the windows,
the scent of reefer on his jacket and tie,
attesting one day that every note
of The Who's *Quadrophenia* could be counted
as a phenomenal masterpiece,
and as implausible as it sounded
I could almost believe.

Bell Telephone Work Gloves

Along with the ragged pea coat
and jaunty fatigue cap
I'd found in the bins at Army Navy,

I wore them each morning
on my paper route: a pair
of my grandfather's work gloves,

admiring their coarse fabric,
those floppy fingers as wide as slats—
cradling flame when I'd light up a smoke.

And how proud in my dexterity—
the tips shiny, ink-smudged—
to pluck each newspaper

from the swaying bag whose
twisted strap dug at my shoulder
down the seedy corridors

of the Garrett House apartments—
to set it carefully
as a platter on a mat;

gaping, as if at a headline,
the day a shape I mistook
for a pile of old bedding

at the end of the hall
moved in its sleep,
my *Inquirer* boy's propriety

unsettled by *who? why?*
as those clownish muffs
went inert at my sides.

Sunday Walkathon

For Dan Kowalski

Spina bifida? The March for Babies?
What did it matter
if I'd taken no pledges—
the whole point to say in school
and to my doubting family
that at least for a day
I'd turned off the TV
just to hike twenty miles,
stretching muscles,
stopping at the little cheering stands
along the way
for my energy bar and juice.

And to be with my friend
under the tall canopy of trees—
to walk and talk,
then go at a trot, weaving
among the crowds of walkers
as we bounced between us
a mottled tennis ball
chewed by a mower,
for a time our volleying
with its crisp punctuation—
one sentence following another—
the only discourse we needed.

In Bob's Garage

For Bob Blaisse and the Guys on Turner Avenue

Too old for tree forts, we still needed a place
where we could drag inside
a sagging couch, a mildewed carpet,
a soda machine loaded for Fridays—
buzzing in the corner on six-packs of Schlitz.
Just a place after school
where we could crank up the turntable:
Bowie Live and Mott the Hoople,
Tull's Ian Anderson with his audacious flute.
A place of refuge where nicknames were conferred:
Snake and Chimpo, Quinny and Nunce,
where we could grow
into our bodies, the adult practices
of drinking and smoking, of telling stories—
that time with new permits,
where along the rafters
lines of beer cans from every state
were like cars in a convoy, ready to roll.

City Church Bells at Dusk

Last hours, late chores,
and the deejay
at Most Blessed Sacrament
has caught the mood
of the city between
supper and sleep—
dropping the needle
on his LP of meandering
tunes to accompany
the fleshy-armed baker
with her leftover hamantash;
the bent-backed shoeshine man
as he puts away
his polish and brushes—
fastens the padlock
of his shingled hut.

Over the lichen-covered
tombstones at Mount Moriah,
the baseball field
at Myers Recreation
where the red-shirted Warriors
are playing the blue-shirted Spartans
a calmness descends,
the city in reverie
as light fades on
the squatting catcher,
on pitcher and batter
before windup and stance.

And on the myopic right fielder
who like a planet out of alignment

is unable to hear
through the cottony bells
the calls of his coaches
as he drifts in his orbit—
at peace in the grass.

On Watching Replays of a Pitcher Struck in the Face by a Comeback Line Drive

For Tim, Joe, and John at the Irish Rover

Just once as we sit and talk,
let the pitcher be shown
on these innumerable screens
not heaped like a jacket
barely stirring in the breeze
but with a dazed smile
after the ball whistles past—
hand to his fluttering heart.
Let us not have to look again
at the hitter with his bat
like a discharged weapon;
the gathered infielders
toeing grass after help arrives—
manager and trainer,
crew with a stretcher hustling out.
Restore for a single replay
the game's features that pass us by:
a blown wrapper; the distinct calls
of vendors in the stands;
and during late innings, the leisurely throws
of outfielders warming up
as twilight breaks like a furtive runner.
Let the broadcasters resume jabbering
about useless statistics.
Show the players not reminding us
by their watchfulness in the dugout
of the impossible fragility
of the ulnar ligament or rotator cuff,
but loose and casual, in a fraternal row—
jibing umpires, spitting sunflower seeds.

"Telephone Line"

With WXPN's *Highs in the 70s*
playing on the radio
as I drove home from work,
it was easy to imagine

I could dial up old classmates:
a few of the rowdy ones
who got out of detention
and joined the Marines, the police force;

the ignored and unnoticed,
who slipped away
from their desks by the window,
overcame dread

of public speaking enough to organize
peace marches, or turn up
to sing "hiding on the back streets"
at karaoke nights around town.

Over distances, decades
I could call to mind
Francis Driscoll in his water-stained Wallabees;
Quadrophenia-head Patrick Coughlin

at Friday's Battle of the Bands,
fingers blurred
across the fretboard of his bass;
the ones from homeroom

who have given me pause
at the dish pan, the leaf pile,

settle for a time
like birds on a wire:

Brian P. Cavanaugh,
the defiance in his eyes softening
on page 128 of the yearbook
as I imagine convincing him that March night

to surrender the keys
of his yellow Mustang,
or make him swerve past the pole
going 90 on Blythe.

Lawn Jockey with a Missing Arm

Someone impaired at night
by drink or the weather
must have clipped its arm
when making the turn
in the big SUV
that's parked in the driveway.
Now, like an employee
without benefits,
it remains on the job
in the antiquated uniform—
white breeches and black boots,
blotches on its red vest—
showing us
by its resolute face,
the chipper bill of its cap,
the meaning of duty
and knowing one's place.
With its good arm
it extends the lantern—
operational or not
it's hard to say
when we pass it there
in the light of day.

II. White Rambler

"I found my father when I did my work."
—Theodore Roethke,
Words for the Wind, 1958

Straightening the Garage

Into the midday sun I brought out
bicycles, a mower, a hobbled doll carriage
minus a wheel—an unruly crowd
made to stand on the asphalt
while I expelled swirling dust
with a flattened broom.

Then all of it back, but in assigned places:
hoses and lawn chairs recoiled, re-slung.
Like rigid cadets the rakes and shovels
awaiting inspection: my father
after a second or third can of Pabst
offering that rare praise,
the hand on my shoulder

not sloughed off these early hours
I gaze out the window—
primed with a pencil
in a house with no garage.

In Praise of Deliverymen

For the muted colors
of their daytime pajamas—
Industry's allotting them
brown, olive, navy, gray.
For the abiding fidelity
of their oafish trucks—
free advertising for W. B. Mason,
Roto-Rooter Plumbing & Drain
through the eight-mile backup
on the Turnpike west.
For the nimble two-steppers
who pass us in the fast lanes
of stairs, genuflect
on the scuffed linoleum
of grocery aisles—
for their sacramental touch
in bestowing bread.
For their truncated courtesies
at receptionists' desks—
quick signings, packages
like gifts ferried across the city;
the names we glimpse
on frayed insignias:
Mikes, Bobs, Johns, and Bills
as common as sparrows
that alight, depart.

Soda Machine at the Garrett Road Laundromat

Humming in the corner,
its face lit up,
it seemed happy to see me
as I fed it coins
and barely took in
through the harsh fluorescence
the notched brown tables
and plastic chairs;
a few solitary people
at the odd hour
smoking or reading magazines
while clothes tumbled
in the windows of driers:
plaids, stripes,
the faint percussion
of hooks and buttons
tapping a plaintive beat.
And once in the stillness
a blue denim work shirt
with arms reaching out
to cuff the dark;
and me feeling the jolt
of those first cold sips
of a Frank's Black Cherry
as I resettled the weighty bag
on my shoulder
and went out again,
bearing news.

Stockboy

It was a privilege those first afternoons
to bag groceries for the cashiers
and be sent to shepherd
a herd of carts that had strayed
from the pasture of the parking lot—
carts he found adrift on corners,
left to graze at curbs, against telephone poles.

And later, to have the honor
of going out again in his zippered fleece
to clean up the boxes
the full-timers had been flinging
out the back door and into the driveway—

empty boxes of Contadina Tomato Paste
and Smuckers Jam with broken jars
that brought out the bees
like late bargain hunters to market—
picking over the remnants.

So lucky for him to have been given this job,
his parents reminded him each night at dinner,
when instead of frittering away time after school,
playing touch football with his friends,

he was gaining valuable experience in the workforce,
carrying boxes to the squat compactor
in a dank-smelling shed among mildewed pallets,

glancing skyward every so often
as geese flew by in their straight formations,
the leaders sounding remarkably

like the store manager, honking orders,
with him turning a doleful eye toward the stragglers—
wary and uncertain, awaiting the next turn.

Summer Janitorial

No reason to feel defeated
by these endless rows
of facing lockers
like identical houses
on a winding block.
With the humblest of remedies—
clump of steel wool, sloshing
aluminum bucket of some
spearmint-smelling intoxicant
cut with water and ammonia—
think purger, purifier,
penitent on one knee,
Led Zeppelin's *Physical Graffiti*
on someone's tape player
as you moisten the steel wool
and begin building a rhythm,
intent on obliterating a year's
fingerprints, scuff marks,
abandoned hearts,
the tendons in your wrist
pulsating with industry,
mind lost in the mantra
fresh start, fresh start
for the scrawny and unpopular,
the pages unwritten
on their new spiral notebooks.
And for the bleary-eyed teachers,
who've gone home for summer—
the slate wiped clean.

Cleaners at Lunch

Rose Tree School Cafeteria, Summer 1975

Lebanon bologna, a Tastykake pie—
same excuse for a lunch
my father packed me all year,
I wanted to impress
two of the Task Force crew
with hair past their shoulders,
woofers bleating in the sleek Camaro
that carried them off
to each curfew-less night.

Earlier, a camaraderie among us
as we'd filled our buckets
and groused about management,
the sweltering prison
of school in July.
Like disgruntled penitents
we'd knelt through the morning
before rows of lockers
only to lose ourselves
in the rhythm of labor,
scouring with clumps of steel wool
that shriveled from rubbing,
left welts on our hands.

Now, across the table where they sat
splitting a pizza,
they raised their eyebrows—
gave a little snort I took for a laugh
until one of them cracked,
"The day my old man makes me a sandwich.
He'd eat it first."

Validation

For CFK, LaSalle College Writing Teacher, October 1978

You are coming alive!—
no words more than these,
scrawled above the broken characters I'd typed
on the dry ribbon and sticking keys
of our family's secondhand Royal,
but enough to carry me past the indifferent
fare collector and urine stench at Olney Station—
their dazzling green, the exclamation point
a torch on a swaying subway ride.
How many times would I need to remove
from the canvas army bag
my crinkled story and read the same words
before I'd be convinced
they wouldn't change color or fade
from the pages of Corrasable Bond,
believe they could almost make up for
every muffed fly and fight
I'd backed down from; erase at my shoulder
the hovering presence of the manager at Shop n Bag,
his whiny criticism as I marked labels on cans?
That words could give me license to hum
while rounding carts or mopping in aisle six
a jar of spaghetti sauce bumped from a shelf,
forgetting my mediocre grades, fumbling around girls,
gray suds lapping my sneakers like surf
as I inscribed linoleum
with easy zigzags, loose figure eights.

For the Taciturn Forklift Operator
Who Finally Spoke

Like a put-upon waiter he'd return
with my order—set it down
on a pallet like a teetering tray.
And watch without comment
as I'd demonstrate as if for his tutelage
the rugged art of wrangling
Hammermill stock from platform to van—
hold each carton at arm's width
before lowering it soundlessly,
then flip it forward in bounding steps.

"Hard work in hot weather,"
he offered just once
as I signed the invoice,
taking in with the cracked dry
leather of his brown shoes, the wilted
flower of his curled insignia,
this cool appraisal
as sudden and unexpected
as a solitary raindrop
aslant from the blue.

Van Loading

I might have driven the company's sleek new Ram,
custard-colored, with FM radio,
but went instead for the pockmarked wreck
with rusted wheel wells and banged-up doors,
letting it binge on Hammermill paper
the men riding forklifts
lowered on pallets like teetering plates;
me in a threadbare Unigraphics tee shirt
walking bent-backed inside the dank walls
to stack rows behind the seats,
pile up cartons like extra servings,
work without restraint
until I'd covered the back windows—
depleted myself in the August heat.
And after signing the invoice,
the sweat of my hand curling the page,
move in the cross breeze toward the Schuylkill River
slow, bovine,
on sated groans, the wheezy breathing
of its worn shocks—
tailpipe scraping as we held the road.

In Denim

Monday after the loud Father's Day
bash in his backyard, free
of the plaid shirt, the pleated shorts
his wife picked out at the clothing shop,
he's off at dawn in denim again—
my neighbor in the big work shoes,
all day up and down to ring the rungs
of ladders, splay from scaffolding,
his head haloed in a red bandana.
Around his waist there's weaponry:
the sheathed screwdrivers; a holstered
drill and hammers; swinging loose
at his side the hand with the busted
knuckles, the blackened nails I watched
bludgeon among children and condiments
on a picnic table a row of empty
beer cans; flick butts in the grass;
thump backs, belches; but today
has the hood eased open on his old truck,
his fingers lithe among wires, hoses;
one ear listening as if to muted music
that suddenly disturbs the dawn
with its sweet percussion—has him dancing
back with dainty steps. So good
this life, he thinks, as he speeds
through the county: the early start
with dew on lawns, the cooing doves;
then all morning with his voice chimed
above clanging hammers, wild shrieks
of drills—him bellowing from rooftops
and the sides of buildings: his needs
at the supply store, the sandwich shop,

coining lyrics to songs on the radio—
in a lewd serenade to his buddies below.

Hispanic Roofing Crew

Wanting to befriend them
or to show solidarity—
all the trumped-up talk
about the building of walls—
I step out in a robe
and give a small ambassadorial wave,
but it's already past six
and they're busy
preparing the house
as if for a festival—
propping ladders
and covering windows,
conversing in Spanish
if they speak at all,
one lifting from the bent arm
of the shepherd's hook
a pot of petunias,
another the black wind chimes
whose delicate music
seems as ecumenical a language
as the cooing of doves—
something I can carry
if only for a moment
before I close up the robe
and go back inside.

Proselytizer, Late Lunch

In a brown fringe jacket,
the beard and placard
like the props of an extra
in a biblical epic,
he's done the work
of hollering himself hoarse
on the corner of Chestnut
at the lunchtime crowd
that rushes past him—
like water parting
around a stump in a stream.

Now, after two at the food court,
he sits at a table
with coffee and a sandwich,
reading glasses low
as he follows the verses
of *The Daily News.*
How strange to find him here—
transformed before our eyes
from crazed city prophet
to worker at rest
with his placard put up,
his bible beside the packets of condiments
by the side of his plate.

Santa, Delayed

By mid-February all the ornaments
on Wyandotte Street have been put away
except for a giant Santa at the corner house.
Driving by I glimpse him at the chimney top
in his wrinkled valor,
empty sack slung over one shoulder
as if waiting for the sleigh to pick him up.

It was weeks ago that the rest of us,
bloated on craft beer and fruitcake,
returned to the construction site
and to the blank faces of our monitors,
but here he is as if emerging in the gray weather,
assaulted by sleet and bird droppings,
causing us to wonder if his team
has played a prank and left him behind,
or if he has been sidetracked all this time
by a family with zesty snacks
and a robust entertainment center.

Easy to picture him with his lips moving,
rehearsing excuses for Mrs. Claus,
but what to tell the young elves—
enterprising designers and assemblers, impressionable interns—
for whom he should be setting an example?

Already he has missed the post-holiday blues party
and the chance to extend along with the bonus checks
a few attaboys to the unsung heroes in Packaging.

Missed, too, the postmortem in the conference room
dubbed The Workshop

where the department heads gather annually
for a long PowerPoint on the past season's highlights,
emphasizing the positive,
though touching on what they might have done better.

And moving forward, as they like to say,
how they might exceed this year's target goals
regarding production, deliverables—
the Wow factor.

Face

All day the face catches itself
in the gaze of sudden mirrors—
running in the watery windows of trains,
or, held in the ponderous yawn
of an elevator, composing its features
as the slow jaws close.
In the still pond of the copier
it commiserates with the sagging
shoulders, comporting itself against
the droning of data; slick pitches
and proposals; the endless duplication
of minutes constrained in a swollen clip.
Which is why the ear, in a day's dwindling
hours, loiters at the hushed peripheries
of cubicles and conference rooms, gathering
small windfalls of gossip; and why the dulled
head lifts as if to music to each creaking
chair and footstep—percussion of the stapler,
cacophony of comma, colon: the hands suspended
above a thicket of dry documents,
surprised in their fluttering from desk to drawer.

Leaving the Editor's Shop

Down the hall they are at it again:
the marketing team with the cuffs rolled
on their good shirts—unskilled, unmuffled,

shouting shop in the big conference room,
revving up points on their sluggish copy—
the main trouble: how to make

this deliverable drivable. How, indeed.
They remember you—quiet shop around the corner;
you in tiny spectacles and that green cardigan

with holey elbows, a few missing buttons,
slumped through seasons over terrible drafts.
Such trust you inspire with your markers, pens,

and little rulers; consulting thick dictionaries
as you strain with deadlines—tinkering,
tweaking in your sensible light.

All morning you take what they give,
then give it back, wordsmithing what's
mangled, misshapen, dropped on your desk;

cleaning up what's piled on the plate;
and afterward, when the last of them
leaves for lunch—partnering their way

out the door—closing shop to comport
yourself in something small, compact,
and economical; companionable

Strunk and White giving guidance
as you weave in traffic; let lines leave
lanes; cruise without deadline, destination—

go tooling along on the open page.

Layoff

Walk it off, my coaches would clap
after the errant pitch
stunned the batter's helmet;
the weak dribbler that rolled
through grass serene as a pond
made its sudden leap for the infielder's chin.

Here among well-meaning colleagues
how fitting it seems
to dispense quips, look past
my drooping desk lamp,
the chipped mug I carry
among my possessions in a carton,

to the glass terrarium that had thrived
on a shelf beside leaning binders,
its ferns composed in fissured dirt,
insouciant leaves waving goodbye.

Old Skills

One by one I'd taken them up
only to set them aside
like tools in a shed left gathering
rust: the day's news

flicked in the dark
toward the blurred target
of a welcome mat; my staccato
bursts with a pricing gun—

slapping labels on cans
like a frenzied drummer
soloing in the aisle.
Gone

my finicky precision
with the pica scale,
the Wite-Out brush,
or today at the Y

after clicking off laps
on a circular track:
before empty bleachers, old
varnish and sweat,

the ball in my hands
as sure as the sun
as it rose, then swooned
in front of the net.

Haircut on My Fortieth Birthday

In a line along the wall
some men sit solemn as jurors
as I squirm through this—

the barber with his deft fingers
pulling the sheet over, tucking
it tight up under my chin.

From a shelf somewhere
top 40 taunts, then comes
a quiet cutting—my hair

in a free fall, slow as snow
drifting down as I watch
it join with other hair, paratrooping

to the floor to form a country
on a map; the stunned shape
of a hunted animal; or one

of those dark, imponderable
clouds that roam overhead to drip
doubt on a day—policing

the treetops; patrolling yards,
small orderly plots; pausing
above the stilled heads and shoulders

of people bowed over mowers,
in the grass with shears
like open mouths—silenced

a moment as the cloud passes over
before they bend back to work
in the laboring light.

White Rambler, Last Ride

After weeks at the curb like a codger
parked in a favorite chair,
it seemed resolved to go on its own—
over potholes, past the drugstore's
prosthetic limbs in the window,
slow, then slower,
in the jolt of bad shocks, bald tires,
my years of neglect.

We rode down 5th past the Olney Colony
and the Portuguese bakery
with its twelve-cent rolls;
past The Church of the Incarnation
to forgive the fickle carburetor
and leak in the windshield.

To remind me with tenderness
of our aimless drives, the sibilance
of trees along the Wissahickon;
nights seeing me home
after pitchers at The Blind Pig,
four in a booth
debating literature and religion,
napkins blotted from Genesse steins.

Under the overpass,
Ed's scrapyard in view,
we went on without flashers
at our decorous pace—
drivers in a procession behind us
not honking, not gesturing
as though out of respect.

III. Brown Duster

Brown Moth on Windshield

Little stowaway behind the left wiper blade,
how I admired your tenacity—
your stick-to-itiveness—
as I flitted on the morning commute
from sports talk to the classical music station,
then back to sports talk after the calamity
of an Eagles' preseason defeat.

Out of the cul-de-sac we drove—
away from the common life
with its dry cleaners and pizza shop,
the deposed kingdom of the video store
still wearing the imprint of its missing sign.

By the time we reached the Turnpike,
I was reflecting on our solidarity:
me with a crick in the neck
and tension in both forearms
as we merged with the tractor trailers;
you full of wanderlust, giving new meaning
to riding shotgun—through the thrill
of buffeting wind.

As traffic slowed and the usual convoy
with Rob's Towing and State Farm Insurance
shuddered past on the shoulder,
I forgot you for a while, grew preoccupied
with deadlines, bulging job jackets,
but when we entered the corporate environs
I couldn't help wondering if you'd embrace
your new surroundings—see them as an idyll
minus cats and floating plastic bags—

or feel as disconcerted as I'd felt
on my first days
when I'd taken in all this sculpted shrubbery,
the line of trees like a welcoming committee,
standing by on their pedestals of dirt.

And all the cars in the parking lot
that had reminded me with mild dread—
or perhaps panic—
of the schoolyard at Most Blessed Sacrament,
the nuns with their clickers,
those perfect formations.

Power Outage After a Storm

"Look for the helpers."
—Mr. Fred Rogers

In our search for coffee we pass the neighbor
whose humming generator closes him off
to the anarchy of the streets:
downed limbs and power lines;
a stockade fence that's quit on diplomacy—
choosing sides in the grass.
Here migratory litter and recycling cans
fleeing the block in their green jumpsuits.
At the corner of Oxford Valley and Olds,
a defective traffic light,
its maimed head in the arms of a tree.

Among the uncaffeinated citizens of the town
(a crowd in mottled fleeces and backwards caps),
we stand in line at The Golden Dawn
as the one waitress on duty
pours coffee at tables,
brings toast and scrambled eggs,
her smile for each patron
like a complimentary mint.
Think of others: volunteers at shelters,
utility crews called up from the Carolinas
on twelve-hour shifts,
the rest of us in some dark advent
moving through our chilled rooms,
or at a strange hour while deep under covers
startled by sudden light.

Brown Duster

Why dwell on its tapping valves
and torn vinyl seats, the dogged engine
that plodded like a work boot?
Easier to think of it as Dusty,
like some spunky mascot on children's television,
good for every adventure
the cast of Little Bears Family Day Care
went on with their crackers and juice.
Behind the bulging eyes of its headlights,
the smiling grill of its mouth,
they'd ride to Briar Bush, the Please Touch Museum,
lively Mrs. Pat at the wheel in her green cap,
and Sarah and Andrew, Elissa and Nick
looking out the windows at cars and trucks,
nature passing like cardboard scenery.
Forget the groaning brakes, its little shudder,
the deposits of oil it left by the curb.
Forget the repair shop at 6th and Tabor,
the rueful mechanic shaking his head.
They were seasons away from the final episodes,
the children grown gangly for their roles
and old Dusty retired in a lot
enduring in memory's reruns.

Crossing State Line

In the dentist's waiting room
I breeze through the A's
on the medical form—
no anemia, no asthma—
as if acing a test.
But when I come to cancer
the chained pen
hesitates over the little box,
and I'm reminded all at once
of trips on the Turnpike:
those long stretches
when lulled by the engine,
some jazz on the radio,
I pass the same
barns, haystacks, abundant trees
that sway at roadside
like an amiable citizenry—
bid farewell, then hello
as I cross the state line.

For My Troubled Prostate, St. Peregrine Arrives

St. Peregrine, patron saint who watches over patients with cancer

When he came on a Tuesday
with some floppy circulars
and appeals for money,
I wasn't impressed so much
by his haloed head,
nor even by the healed foot
he displayed under robes,
but just by the fact
that he turned up at all:
tiny figurine,
this humblest of gifts purchased
at a Catholic supply store
and, like a martyr
for a cause, Scotch-taped
to the note my uncle sent—
for a moment
the skeptic in me quieted
as I freed him from his bindings,
then assigned him to the province
of the desk where under
the penitential bow
of a gooseneck lamp
he ministered each morning
to the rites of pencils—
stubbed, faith-worn, nodding amen.

Dumpster Diving

My son on a late-night raid
brings home spotted bananas,
two gallons of organic whole milk
that lapsed on the shelf,
the loot in red saddlebags
he's secured to his bike—
courier of the outdated and overripe.
I come downstairs in the morning
to find in the crowded refrigerator
a spoiled cauliflower
and a convention of carrots;
on the table I'd wiped clean
wilted kale and molting onions;
among tools in the shed
dented soups, a frozen pizza—
all of it
having me turn in politeness
as I'd done mornings after parties
when friends slept over,
faintly repulsed by their disheveled state.

It's what months of touring on a brown bicycle
has taught, I suppose:
the importance of living frugally;
of accepting after miles of hills,
of squinting over a laminated map,
what sustenance a dumpster provides.

And what I who crave order
(yet can recognize pluck)
have tried to embrace
during my grown son's visits:

scattered clothes and bike paraphernalia;
beside the kale and onions
suspect zucchini, a jovial squash,
everything waiting for my son
to appear with knife and cutting board
as if to rouse them for a festival—
the big stir-fry—
but for now, like crashers at a club,
blocking my view of that classic ensemble
of salt and pepper, the sugar between,
all three, as it turns out,
only too eager to give up on decorum—
to step down from their humble stage of cork,
the pepper already on its side,
surrendering itself.

Suburban Daughter on an Urban Farm

"Grow a garden, grow a community."
Feedom Freedom; Detroit, Michigan

Sitting with coffee at the kitchen table,
I see under the brown compost
in the backyard a green shoot
that comes out straight, then veers
toward Detroit where our suburban daughter
tends her chores on a farm.
Strange to think of her there,
this girl of ours once stretched out
in the long canoe of the couch—
adrift on *Dawson's Creek*—
now weeding and watering
with her compatriots of the soil,
volunteers like herself
who have learned the language
of sustainability and soup kitchens:
the urban lot. Who can know
which way a child will go?
Between dilapidated buildings
on a snug half-acre—
a transplant flourishing
with cilantro, arugula, dill, and kale.
In a distant city, across state lines
to hoe and till in a sweat-stained hat
and mud-caked clodhoppers—
in borrowed duds she's made her own.

Driving by Grounds for the New Lowe's

Above some straggly grass
and blown litter
it waved at the traffic
from a chain-link fence—
wobble-headed baby doll
in a pink jumper
marking this site
of cranes and porta potties,
John Deere excavators
in the rutted dirt.

A prank, I supposed,
on driving by,
but when I reached the light
I wondered who among
the crew in hard hats—
young father, grudging foreman—
might have taken the trouble
to recover it from the sidewalk
and secure it with care
at a child's eye level—
saving it from abandonment
with no thought of reward.

Saturday Chores with Jehovah's Witnesses

The first mild weekend, and in their dark attire
they start down the block
like something shaken from a can,
dispersing onto the row house porches,
proclaiming to the citizens of Olney
that they are free to put up their toilet brushes,
their rags and cleanser—
that world's end is at hand.
Behind parted curtains I vacillate,
as always, between listening with forbearance
and staying out of view,
sorry for the children, dragged along in their miniature suits,
yet envious of such certitude,
a glow no curt remark, no slammed door
can extinguish, the vacuum wailing
as I remember from my catechism
that envy is one of the seven deadly sins,
God with a green marker,
finding my name in the thick ledger
He keeps for venial infractions,
making His precise mark before closing the heavy cover,
dust motes swirling like purgatorial souls.

Failed Short Stories

In a scuffed metal file cabinet that sits
catty-corner in our mud room,
they dwell among expired warranties,
instructions for discarded appliances,
scenes once bustling with industry
haunting me like factories glimpsed
from a train window—
weeds strewn through abandoned lots.
What became of their people—
the old couple greeted each morning
by the stifling air of their thrift store
like a wet dog roused from a carpet;
the inept husband stranded
on a step ladder in the bathroom,
dangling socket in his hand?
Too late to resolve their conflicts—
the disputes over parking,
a parishioner's harbored resentments.
No use going back to alter a gesture
or amend what was said.
You must watch your tendency to lollygag,
a helpful editor once scrawled on a rejection,
which had me pondering *lollygag,*
its cartoonish syllables
before returning to characters
whose lives I'd imagine:
brick layers and curbside painters,
a crotchety neighbor from my childhood
who sharpened blades in his cellar,
describing him with the fixation of a poet
at the expense of plot—
of narrative pace—

as he stood in the hysterical shriek of machinery,
the two of us disappearing in a shower of sparks.

The Norton Reader
"The door's locked from the inside."
—Nar-Anon saying

Like a scared recruit
my son boards his flight

to the Florida rehab,
and as I walk back to the car

I find glittering on the asphalt
among anonymous bumpers

a baggage lock
with the key inside—

returning me
to the thin pages

of that fat anthology
when I'd pick up on symbols

that authors would scatter
like colored eggs;

me with my industrious pen
and blue spiral notebook,

eager in class to show off
my insight—

to open a discussion
about fictional lives.

Cleaning Up After the Nar-Anon Family Group Meeting

Doing service, we call it,
but it's nothing, really—
no more than the courtesy
of guests after a party
that prompts us
to gather up the folding chairs
or tend to the coffee,
a few stiffened Fig Newtons
on a paper plate.

And in the dim light
of this church basement
to find ourselves glancing back
for stray cups and crumpled napkins,
postponing it would seem
before someone hits the switch
the moment we adjust
scarfs and hats
and like passengers on a train—
stiff and bleary
after telling our stories—
nod cordially, then allow our faces
to become inscrutable
as we disperse in the parking lot
to separate cars.

"Old Man"

For Andrew, six months in recovery, Spring 2011

As you strain for the high notes,
I want to imagine it's the 1970s
and I am brooding with Neil Young
at the wistful campfire of the turntable—
worn grooves like crackling embers—
and not gazing at palm fronds
on a wall in Delray.

But from identical chairs
we watch you at the foot of our bed—
guitar and sandals,
a crew cut that brings back the boy
with his baseball cards
those days before court dates, trips
to detox, the resolve in your eyes,
unwavering pitch on the words
Twenty-four and so much more
enough for us to believe
in the transcendent power
of songs played on a dust-clumped needle—
our hearts like old vinyl, skipping again.

"Magic on East Monmouth Street"

Prevention Point Philadelphia Block Party, October 2018

How well you wear the worn accoutrements
of untucked flannel and turned-around cap—
the bearded troubadour
with your back to the wall of this converted church.
But as I watch you with guitar and amp,
I'm thinking not of magic, but of the actual
miles that brought you here:
after rehab six months on the road
with provisions mounted to a Raleigh tour bike—
across state lines with laminated maps.
The long practice of Vipassana meditation.
At Hurricane Flats, the disciplined farm hand
like a penitent on his knees—
picking potatoes in a Vermont sun.

And now a case worker yourself,
competing on this closed-off city block
with tarot card readers, pamphleteers
for an audience of sanctuary seekers
too jittery, it seems, to be fixed in place—
your voice, in a conjurer's trick, disappearing
when high on the trestle above Kensington Avenue
the El rumbles past,
and then, like hope, rises again.

At Five Points

Frost contended with two roads diverging in a yellow wood,
but imagine my quandary at the juncture of Five Points
as I sat at the light in a dented Corolla.
Saturday errands, and sorry I couldn't be five people,
or a plucky task force of six or eight,
I wondered after returning some books to the library
if I should take the hard left
past the island of pumps at the struggling Mobil
or the easy right that would bring me to Acme
with its well-trodden aisles. Too early
for a jaunt down the road to McManus's Beef & Ale.
How long to decide before the light turned green
and the drivers behind me
(many who had never read Frost)
leaned on their horns to nudge me along?

In the shimmering sun a girl's softball team
held signs for a car wash, and embarrassed
to have depleted my cash on fines at the library,
I took the road past some obscure law offices
and the quirky shop that would repair your bicycle
and try to sell you a vacuum,
the proprietor affable in a gray work shirt,
cap tilted back on his head,
demonstrating among frames, new rubber tires
the prowess of the orange Royal
(the only model he sold)
as it gorged on scraps he scattered on a runner,
the greedy abandonment of its lit face
enough to illuminate an entire Saturday—
to awaken all five of my senses—
as I made my way home.

After Writing

I return the pencil to its place
on the sidelines, but in helmet
and jersey it comes jogging back,
breaking from its teammates—
smudged eraser, gooseneck lamp—
like the player on the squad
who refuses to quit. Game over,
I can conjure up nothing more
than to jot on a scrap
eggs, butter, flour, bread,
thinking all the while
of the orange and yellow peppers,
emerging from the spray
of their morning shower—
plump and nubile, with glistening skin.

Before the Eagles Game

It was safe to say
as I shopped at Acme
for cold cuts and chips
that the artesian loaves
on a rack by the deli
gave me no urge
before the stunned crowd
of Sunday shoppers
to connect on a slant route
with a man in a jeff cap
as he pushed his cart
toward the end zone
of the checkout.

And that I felt no flutter
on passing #20
(a bit paunchy in his jersey)
as he stood fixated
at the meat case—
wholly in the moment
of surveying steaks.

Behind the store a row of bales
against the stucco wall
bore no resemblance
to the immutable force
of an offensive line,
nor did some bees I glimpsed
whooping it up
over produce boxes
piled in the driveway
put me in mind

of the Steelers' cheerleaders—
in their detestable colors
of black and gold.

No football zealot,
no bleeder of green,
I could say with conviction
that a formation of geese
I saw flying above me
just minutes before kickoff at 4:25
did not quicken my pulse,
nor seem anything at all
like the Eagles players
led by their quarterback
as they streamed across
the field of the sky.

86th Birthday

In companion seating at the Phillies game,
my father is never alone,
never unattended—
my brothers and I bringing beer
from the concession stand,
his copilots through the turbulence
of rock and PhanaVision,
the innings he dozes with runners on base.

Such fuss, he says with a rueful sigh,
the red birthday balloon the folks
at Continuing Care had fastened
to his wheelchair for the night out
a flare for well-wishers:
the Phillies Go Green Patrol,
a silver-haired ambassador
with a tan, bestowing a new baseball,

and all the while I'm remembering a Saturday
in my boyhood I watched from the window
as he sat in the garage with a can of Pabst.
A light rain was falling,
and across the pond of the driveway,
in a lawn chair after chores,
he was like a man inhabiting his own continent,
neutral, and at peace,
removed from the squabbles over television—
the small flare-ups inside the house.

Towhead

Through the turnstile we went—
grown sons shepherding father,
a red birthday balloon
fastened to the wheelchair
with a piece of string
drawing as if to a flag
salutes from well-wishers
ferrying hot dogs and beer.

And all through the game
our dad the celebrity
with his boy's balloon,
receiving from a Phillies ambassador
a fist bump and a new ball;
more smiles from fans;
then, in the late innings,
this towheaded kid
with his splash of freckles,
hair fine as silk
from Nebraska corn.

Standing with his mother,
he waited for a sign
before coming forward
like Whitey Ashburn
in his rookie days
to lay down his sacrifice:
a pristine dollar
on the arm of the chair.

Saturday Dances

All his life my father moved
from task to task—
sweeping in with the groceries,
or making graceful turns
across the living room carpet
with his squat partner—
the dented Electrolux—
to their song of household dust.

How different that Saturday
we returned from shopping
to find the empty wheelchair
with its arms reaching out,
and him like a novice,
improvising steps
after sliding to the floor—
new partner, new dance.

My Father's Farewell

The SEPTA paratransit van waits at the curb
while my father in his wheelchair
telegraphs with a sly smile
that half-wave, half-salute—
like the president boarding Air Force One.

Always these days at the end of the party
this little joke that never fails
to win a laugh, the whole family
come out to say goodbye—
assembled on the lawn
like an audience at a club;

and my father, that serious man
who all his life had taught
the value of keeping busy
with routine chores—
the vacuuming, the mowing,
quick trips to the store—

now resolute in a chair,
a teacher still as he plays
for us the rueful comedian
with his driver as straight man—
giving infirmity a parting jab.

Winter Coat Pocket

For Patricia, 35-year wedding anniversary

Each winter I recover from the closet
that navy wool coat
with its pills and loose buttons,
my rummaging hand
dredges last year's debris:
old receipts and lip balm,
the ingredients for corn chowder
in a seabed of lint.

And these forest green mittens
with holes in both thumbs:
Not crammed in a drawer
nor in the distant towns
of separate pockets,
but as a conjoined couple
weathering seasons—
nestled away in the dark.

Meeting My Creative Writing Teacher in the Afterlife

For Claude Francis Koch

Each morning I summon you up, my devoted teacher,
returning to your cramped office in Olney Hall
where I can smell the corn cob, be awed
by the industry of your messy desk.

In those days it was enough for me
to turn in stories for our biweekly conferences,
the two of us following in the margins
your penciled notations I thought of as rails—

no, make that ladders on a job site,
resting against my paragraphs,
thick spackling with words,
characters muddling in unfinished rooms.

Such faith you had in me, yet who would have guessed
I'd abandon my stories with their distant paydays
to put poems together like a village of condos
or health care offices near a suburban mall.

What will you say when we meet?
I sometimes wonder—
that I should have taken up Mel Bay's easy guitar chords,
caught more Phillies games on TV?

Or, perhaps like a hotel clerk,
you'll glance tactfully away while signing me in,
cordial as I stand with my family of poems—
loose, shambling, in casual clothes.

Recognizing that travelers come from all over—
expansionist novelist, poet tending
a fenced city lot—
you'll direct me to my fusty room overlooking the highway
where I will find by the made bed with its reading lamp
the standard desk with pen and tablet,
packets of some generic coffee,
phone at my bedside,
flash of the occasional wake-up
reminding me of your scrawled "Writing?"
on Christmas cards—
the only attention I'll need.

Joseph A. Chelius works as an editorial director for a health care communications agency in the suburbs of Philadelphia. His work has appeared in *Commonweal, Christianity & Literature, Poetry East, Poet Lore, Rattle, The American Journal of Poetry,* and other journals. His first full-length collection of poems, *The Art of Acquiescence,* was published by Word Poetry in 2014.